D1711713

Morrie Turner

Creator of "Wee Pals"

by Mary Kentra Ericsson

CHILDRENS PRESS®
CHICAGO

PICTURE ACKNOWLEDGMENTS

AP/Wide World Photos—2
Cartoon on page 7 courtesy of Bil Keane
Photographs and cartoons provided by Morrie Turner—8, 27,
28 (2 photos), 29 (3 photos), 30 (photo and 3 cartoons), 31 (2 photos),
32 (1 photo), 33 (4 cartoons), 34 (2 photos), 44 (2 photos), 56,
64 (photo and 3 cartoons), 76, 88, 95, 96 (4 cartoons), 100
Cartoons on pages 30, 33, 64, and 96 reprinted with permission of
News America Syndicate
Cover illustration by Len W. Meents

Library of Congress Cataloging in Publication Data
Ericsson, Mary Kentra.
    Morrie Turner, creator of "Wee pals."

    (People of distinction)
    Includes index.
    Summary: Relates how a talented black boy in California,
encouraged by sympathetic teachers, turned his interest in
drawing into a career as a successful and popular syndicated
cartoonist.
    1. Turner, Morrie—Juvenile literature. 2. Cartoonists—
United States—Biography—Juvenile literature. [1. Turner,
Morrie. 2. Cartoonists. 3. Afro-Americans—Biography]
I. Title. II. Series.
PN6727.T87Z67 1986   741.5'092'4 [B] [92]   85-30846
ISBN 0-516-03222-4

Table of Contents

FOREWORD

In the cast of "The Family Circus" I occasionally include a playmate of Billy, Dolly, and Jeffy's. His name is Morrie and he is modeled after Morrie Turner, the subject of this book.

My cartoon character looks somewhat like the real-life Morrie, but not exactly. The cartoon version is better looking— and much younger! The pen and ink Morrie is six or seven years old and cute. The real one is a hundred and ten and resembles Uncle Remus.

I'm really not sure of that age, but I do know that this lovable cartoonist, who is a dear friend, aged considerably during a wartime tour we did together in Vietnam entertaining the troops. Come to think of it, so did I. And his drawing style changed during our visits to the battlefronts. He drew with a quivery line. So did I.

Morrie has been an outspoken pioneer in the integration struggle and a crusader. His innovative "Wee Pals" strip is a personal favorite of mine.

He has called to the nation's attention the long list of black people recognized for their brilliant accomplishments in many fields.

In the field of cartooning Marvelous Morrie heads that list.

Bil Keane

©CSI

Morrie entertains some of his nieces and nephews

Chapter 1

A NAME OF YOUR OWN

Seven-year-old Morrie was too excited to stand still that morning in 1930 when Mama told him and his brothers, Jay, Marion (nicknamed Buster), and Ed to stand in line in front of her for inspection.

"Tie your shoestrings, Morrie," she ordered.

"And you, Jay," she instructed Joseph, "put your shirttails in your pants.

"Edward, even if your hair is curly, it needs a comb and brush once in a while. I want all of you to look respectable when you go to meet your father at the station. Not like a pack of wild Indians."

"Whoever heard of black Indians?" Morrie laughed.

"Guess you'll be drawing that tonight," Jay grinned at

Morrie who was searching in his pocket for a pencil.

Mama kept on looking at them sternly. "Do what I say, then you can go to the Sixteenth Street station to meet your father when the train comes. And maybe, if you behave, he'll let you ride with him to the Oakland mole."

Anxious to go to the tunnellike building where the trains were cleaned before their next trip, Morrie tied his shoelaces in a firm knot, then watched his brothers while Jay tucked in his shirt, Buster brushed his pants, and Ed smoothed his hair with his hands.

"All right, now walk like gentlemen and watch your little brother," Mama warned the older boys.

When she turned to go back into the two-story wooden house where they lived, the boys broke into a run, Morrie panting to keep up. He could see the heels and soles of his brothers' shoes lifting as they ran, their faces turned toward him as they yelled, "Hurry, Shrimp." Maybe he was the smallest, but he could run just as fast as they could; well—almost, Morrie told himself.

A "too-too-toot" of the train whistle urged the boys to a faster pace. "It's Dad's train and it will be stopping for a few minutes at the tracks in the depot," Morrie thought.

His father and the other porters would come hurrying with baggage carriers that looked like fenced platforms on two wheels, Morrie knew. He had seen it many times. There would be people crowding close to the smoking black engine, waving and calling to their friends who were getting off the train.

Panting, Morrie and his brothers stood at the edge of the crowd, impatient for the people to get off the train, and for the porters to get them routed to waiting taxis and streetcars. The friends and relatives who had come to meet them would leave then, too.

The engine started chugging again as the boys ran to Car 14, knowing that their father's shining face would grin a welcome to them as he waited at the Pullman doors.

"Hi, fellas. Who wants a ride to the mole?"

The boys raced to the metal step-up stool still on the ground beside the train, reaching high with their feet to touch the first step.

"One, two, threeee, up you come. Be careful," Dad warned. "Now inside, quick, before the train starts." Dad helped Morrie first as the older boys scrambled up to the platform after him.

Already the train was starting to move forward, its huge iron wheels hissing as they turned on the tracks, while smoke flew from the engine, and the whistle's shriek cut through the twilight sky.

Morrie and his brothers sank into the deep red velvet seats of the Pullman car, the two smaller ones pressing their noses against the window as the train started. San Francisco Bay was ahead. Morrie sniffed deeply, feeling the damp fog, the smoke, and the upholstery dust getting into his nostrils.

"Back to the sleepers, Morrie, Jay, Buster, Ed," Dad pulled at the boys' arms.

It felt good to have Dad giving orders for a change, Morrie thought. It took his father three days to get to Chicago, and three days to come back, so Mama was boss while he was gone. She would bake light, golden biscuits and pancakes, and she was forever scrubbing clothes and making the boys go to church with her.

But Dad looked big, exciting, and strong, Morrie thought as he feasted his eyes on him, feeling warm and glad to have him home again.

"If you boys are real empty inside, we can stop in the diner and maybe get some pie or something to eat," Dad smiled at them. This was part of his homecoming they loved.

Meanwhile the train heaved and clattered toward the mole, the great canopied building near San Francisco Bay, where ferryboats churned back and forth between Oakland and San Francisco.

For Morrie, this was the best part of meeting Dad. He felt

like a traveler himself, almost as if he were going to Chicago or some other end of the earth. Mama had been places. She had graduated from Southern University in 1904 and had been a nurse and taught school in New Orleans and other places in Louisiana, so she knew about going places. But Morrie hadn't been anywhere but Oakland since he was born there December 11, 1923.

"Gee, Dad," he said, tugging at his father's jacket, "when I grow up I'm going to be a porter, just like you."

"Dammit, boy, shut up with talk like that," Pa exploded. "I don't want my kids to be porters. Everybody calls porters George. That's not my name. I've got one of my own. It's James Edward Turner." Dad was shouting. "You're Morrie, and you're Joseph, and you're Marion, and you," he jabbed his finger at each of them, shaking with anger, "you're Edward. And you're going to be something where people call you your own name."

Dad's forehead was wrinkled and his fists were clenched. The boys looked at him in wonder. What's all this fuss about a name?

"Yep, mine's Morrie," his youngest son nodded, putting his hand in his father's. He knew Dad's temper was like a match. It flared up and in a second it was gone. "I'm going to sign Morrie all over my drawings when I'm a cartoonist."

13

As far back as he could remember, Morrie always was drawing.

"Hadn't anyone told you, black boys don't be artists? They work for other folks," his grandmother often said.

Stopped in his daydreaming, Morrie looked up at his father again. Dad didn't seem all muscle and magic anymore. He only looked old and tired. Morrie noticed for the first time the white streaks in Dad's short black hair.

"Let's go home and see what your Mama's got for dinner. You guys can run ahead and tell her we're coming," Dad told his older boys. "Morrie and I'll be along in a few minutes. I'm going to buy all the Sunday papers—the *Tribune*, the *Examiner*, and the *Chronicle*—so you kids can have the funnies, if Morrie doesn't scribble his drawings all over them before you get your turn to read them."

He patted Morrie on the head. Dad's anger of the moment before was forgotten. Morrie thought being the youngest in the family wasn't too bad.

Morrie enjoyed having his dad at home, but he never seemed to stay long enough.

"You keep that chile tied to your apron strings," a neighbor, Mrs. Jackson, told Mama that sunny Saturday morning after Dad had gone.

14

Morrie handed his mother clothespins as she hung the rows of pants, stockings, underwear, towels, and sheets on the line.

"The others disappear and I need someone to go to the store and sweep the yard and do something to help," Mama answered.

Morrie really didn't mind helping. His brothers were always in a rush to be off somewhere without him.

"Like he had the measles or something to catch," Mama complained.

There were lots of other kids in the Tenth and Kirkham Street neighborhood where they lived. Even if none of them were around, Morrie always found something to do.

"It's like he has a playmate in his head," Mama told Grandma when she was visiting them from Natchez, Mississippi. "I never know what it'll be next. Last Saturday—"

Morrie still felt the heat on the bottom of his pants, from what had happened last Saturday.

Jay had brought a big, heavy book home from school.

"For homework," his brother said, but he never did open the covers.

Morrie played with the book whenever he had a chance. He balanced it on his head pretending he was on a high tightrope instead of treading the lines of the cement backyard. When the book toppled from his head and he caught it, Morrie breathed a sigh of relief.

"Treat books nice and gentle, like the preacher does," Mama scolded.

"Yea, like this." Morrie opened the book and held it close to his face. He jumped to the front porch and yelled, "Brethern and Sistern, come you if ye wishes to be saved. Let me tell you about the devil and his works, how hellfire burns those who sin."

The neighborhood kids circled on the pavement below. Windows in the houses nearby opened and heads popped out.

"Let me save you, brothers and sisters," Morrie yelled louder, enjoying his bigger audience. "I'll tell you how, and pass the collection plate." He grabbed a saucer from under Mama's geranium pot.

Bam! Out of nowhere, it seemed, the palm of Mama's hand met the seat of Morrie's pants. He popped to the ground pretending she had smacked him down.

"What would the minister think of you if he heard this, and me, your mother, the president of the Baptist Ladies' League?" Mama's eyes bulged with anger as the kids circling the yard yelled, "Save us, Morrie, save us," hoping the game would keep on.

"Scat. Go home. All of you." Mama yelled. "And you! You."

She shook with anger as she faced Morrie. "I should skin you. Just for what you did, you'll go to bed right now, before dark, and kneel and say your prayers first. Ask the Lord to forgive you and help you to be good enough, so when you grow up, maybe you could be a preacher. An honest, real one, talking in a chapel, not yelling from a porch."

Morrie wished now that he had played sea captain instead of preacher. Often the railing on the porch was his ship, and he was the captain, leading his men on rough voyages, while he rocked and swayed on bended knees. Or he and the neighborhood kids would use the basement for a clubhouse, and Morrie would be "teacher" and show them how to draw.

"To the bathroom and bed," Mama roared hearing the neighbor kids still tittering. "I just hope the reverend doesn't hear about this. If he does you'll get some more pants warming," she promised, waving the palm of her hand at him.

Morrie headed slowly to the bedroom he shared with his brothers, glad they weren't home to taunt him about being a baby, put to bed early. As he pulled the sweater over his head and peeled out of his pants, Morrie shrugged his shoulders. He'd have time to play his favorite game even if the boys did come home. He knew Mama wouldn't let them in the room until bedtime since he was being punished.

All the two-story wooden houses in the neighborhood were

close together, their walls almost touching. Morrie was glad the kids next door weren't home, because if the windows were open you could hear voices.

Getting into his pajamas, Morrie reached under Jay's pillow for his brother's flashlight. Then he crawled under the bed for the roll of wrapping paper he had begged from the butcher when he went to get meat for Mama. He dug under his pillow for pencils and crayons.

Morrie draped the blankets from the bed until they reached the floor. He lay on his stomach and propped up the lighted flashlight on the mattress. A circle of light flooded in an arc on the floor.

Morrie spread the paper on the floor and put his crayons and pencil near him. Now he had a studio of his own. He could draw for hours without anyone bothering him. He'd do pictures of movie stars—maybe one of James Cagney because Dad looked like him. And when Mama got over being mad at him, he'd give it to her to put on the dining room wall with the other drawings she had saved.

Chapter 2

SCHOOL DAYS

Going to grade school wasn't so bad, Morrie thought that fall morning as he walked three blocks to Cole School. He liked people around him, and from all directions in West Oakland boys and girls walked or ran to the school grounds. If they came early they could play a game of marbles or have a few trys at handball or a quick game of "run-sheep-run."

Coming from Morrie's neighborhood were Gus and Nick, whose parents were Greek. There was Charlie, their Chinese friend (some of the other kids called him "Chink," but Mama wouldn't allow name-calling). Pedro, whose father was a Mexican laborer, came from the train yards; Al, their Portuguese friend, shambled by; and Paul, their white neighbor, followed.

"Like a patchwork quilt," he heard his teacher Mrs. Bullock describe her pupils to the principal. "Every color, every kind. I just hope they learn to read," she sighed.

Morrie didn't worry much about reading. It was drawing he wanted to learn. How to make bodies of ballplayers. How to show animals running. How to make bonfire smoke curl into the sky and disappear while the flames went down. Which end did you start with, the sky or the ground? Morrie wondered that morning in the crowded classroom.

A ruler banging against his knuckles made Morrie realize he was supposed to be working. Mrs. Bullock looked big and angry as she stood over him. "This is spelling, not dreaming time. Now pick up your pencil and get ready to write some of your spelling words."

Morrie picked up the tooth-marked yellow pencil that was only an inch-long stub.

"Hold it between your thumb and forefinger, not your middle finger," Mrs. Bullock said, her voice louder with each word. "How many times have I told you that? You'll never learn to write legibly, if you hold your pencil in such a clumsy way."

Morrie shifted the pencil to his thumb and forefinger, but it went clattering down the aisle. "I just can't seem to hold it like that, teacher. It rests so easy on this bigger finger." He picked up his pencil. "Just look, teacher." With flashing movements Morrie drew the figure of a cat. "See how easy it goes?" he grinned.

"I said spelling time. The word c-a-t, not a picture. I swear, Morrie, you'll never know how to write anything but your name if you don't do what you're told. Don't you want to be something some day?"

"Yes, Ma'm. Jack Armstrong, the guy on radio. He can do anything."

"But you're Morrie Turner and the first thing you have to do is learn to read and write, and add two and two."

So again Morrie picked up the pencil. "Yes, teach', Ma'm."

It seemed that way all through school for Morrie. No matter which class he was in, no matter what he was supposed to be studying—geography or English—he saw it in pictures; the teacher's mouth open in different positions; the kids slouched at their desks.

But Morrie had to admit he needed word learning too. Especially in the four-page *Neighborhood Nooz* that Morrie wrote every Saturday. He drew pictures of his friends, wrote about what they were doing, who hit the most runs, and listed the names of new people who moved to their street. He sold his "paper" to the neighbors for a nickel.

"I'm in business," he told his dad proudly.

But report card time at school was a bad time for Morrie. "Wait until your dad sees your marks," his mother would scold. "No more crayons for you till you get better grades."

Morrie was learning the joy of swiftly sliding crayons over paper, making different colors bring a face alive: yellow, black, and brown ones. He drew most evenings instead of doing homework. When Mama questioned him about school, Morrie had a quick answer. "Gee, Mama, I'm good at football. Know how many touchdowns I made?"

"Never mind football, or drawing; put your nose in a schoolbook for a change. I don't want you in trouble like other kids around here, breaking windows and clouting cars." Mama looked worried. The older boys were out and she had heard police whistles screeching. The lines in her forehead only smoothed out when all the boys were home.

"After homework, can I draw then?" Morrie begged.

"And what are you doing now?" Mama wanted to know.

"A football picture. And know what? I'm going to show it to Mr. Spencer, the principal. He doesn't laugh at my drawings," Morrie told his mother.

Remembering how he had seen the cartoonist (Bill Holman) draw "Smokey Stover" in a movie, Morrie pushed his soft pencil quickly from one position to another until he finally had a whole team playing, every man in action. Before school the next morning, Morrie timidly tapped at Mr. Spencer's office door. The principal opened it and smiled at Morrie.

"You can't be in trouble before school starts. What's the matter today?"

"I just got something for ya'," Morrie stammered. "Something I made at home last night. I thought maybe you'd like to see it." Slowly he unrolled the butcher paper and laid his drawing on the principal's desk. Mr. Spencer peeked over Morrie's shoulder at the drawing. Then he pushed him aside. Now I've done it again, Morrie thought to himself, churning inside. First the teacher gets mad at me, then Ma. Now its the principal.

Mr. Spencer wheeled around and faced Morrie, his face alight with a broad smile. "Say Morrie, that's good. May I keep this one? I'd like to put it on the wall in back of my desk so everyone coming in can see it." Morrie nodded, too happy to talk. "And would you put your name on it?" This must be a dream, Morrie thought, pinching himself to be sure he was awake. Mr. Spencer was asking for his drawing! "Put your name on it right here in big letters," Mr. Spencer beamed.

With his thumb and his middle finger pressed close, Morrie proudly printed his name. Wait until Dad and Mama and the boys heard.

Morrie made it to junior high, somehow, and he found the work very difficult. Why did a black kid, who wanted to be a cartoonist, have to take Spanish? ¿Cómo está usted? A language with question marks that went upside down. Somehow none of it could get through Morrie's head.

While he was in study hall one day, trying to make the words go from his eyes through his brain, Morrie saw Mr. Morton, the teacher, motion him to come to his desk.

"I'm a friend of Mr. Spencer and he told me you like drawing. Maybe better than Spanish. I have something here I think you might like to see. Have you heard of James Montgomery Flagg, Morrie?"

"Sure," Morrie answered quickly.

Who hadn't heard of Flagg? In almost every newspaper or magazine there were eye-catching drawings of beautiful women by Flagg. His World War I recruiting poster of Uncle Sam and the caption, "I Want You," was thought to be a self-portrait.

"Know how he does this?" Mr. Morton asked, pointing to a magazine cover. "It's with pen and ink. That's the new style that you might want to try. How about taking this book on Flagg I borrowed from the library and studying it at home, after your Spanish? You're good enough with pencils and crayons. Try something new."

Morrie hugged the book under his arm.

And even though he tried harder, Morrie failed Spanish. But it didn't matter too much to him. Now he was learning to use pen and ink for feathery drawings to create a lightness he had never dreamed his fingers could produce. It wasn't the style he liked best, but it was fun to learn that there were other ways to draw.

And now two adult educators believed in him. First the principal, and now a teacher. He'd show them that when it came to drawing he wouldn't always be second.

Even if he weren't a top student, the kids liked Morrie. When it was class election time Morrie was nominated for secretary. All the candidates had to give a speech in assembly, telling why they would be good officers. Morrie had a hard time preparing his speech. He didn't have good grades to brag about. But the kids yelled and clapped for him.

"Draw us a picture, Morrie," they shouted. That's what they liked about him.

When the votes were counted Morrie had edged ahead of the girl with top grades who ran against him; he had won.

When graduation time came, Morrie knew all the class officers had to make a speech during the program in the auditorium, which would be full of parents and friends.

Qualifying for graduation from junior high had been a tough achievement. Morrie had to do extra work on most of his Saturdays to make up graduation requirements.

But graduation day came closer and closer, and none of the teachers asked Morrie to prepare for the program. Passing the auditorium one day, he heard students practicing their speeches. Standing in the back row by the door, Morrie watched. He was class secretary, but the girl who had run against him had been asked to make the speech. When she saw Morrie she started stammering over her lines.

It didn't matter much to Morrie. But why should only white kids be on the program? He'd have to figure out something to tell Mama. She'd already been telling the neighbors her boy was going to be a graduation speaker.

"Look, Mama," he started that night, "don't count on hearing me talk at graduation. Who wants to get up on the stage in front of all those people? The girl who ran against me will do it."

It was just a little lie—a white lie, some people would call it. But for the first time Morrie wondered if the color of his skin would really make a difference in what people would let him do.

The 1929 kindergarten class of Cole Grammar School. Morrie Turner is in the top row, third from the left.

Morrie is sitting behind the drum in this photo taken in 1934 of his music class in Cole School.

Morrie's mother and father, Nora C. and James E. Turner, on the porch of their Berkeley home.

Above: Morrie served in the army during World War II, where he got his start in cartooning.

Right: Sid Shaffer, with Morrie, was the model for "Jerry" in "Wee Pals."

Below: Morrie with his mother and Aunt Sara Williams on their front lawn.

Letha and Morrie at their printing press in the late 1960s. His first cartoon featured the "Dinky Fellas."

Morrie loves to illustrate the art of cartooning to others.

Letha and Morrie with their youngest grandson in the foreground; in the rear are Patricia, Morrie, Jr.'s wife, more grandchildren, and Morrie, Jr.

WEE PALS, viewing the world through the eyes of kids of many different origins, has been so successful in promoting "Rainbow Power" with laughter that Morrie Turner has won a dozen awards from such organizations as the National Conference of Christians and Jews and the B'nai B'rith Anti-Defamation League.

The Turner boys, left to right: Morrie, Joe, Buster, and Ed, pose with their mother about 1934 (above) and again in the same order after World War II (below).

Chapter 3

LEARNING TO WRITE AND TO FIGHT

"How would you like to do some drawing and writing for the school paper, Morrie?"

Morrie looked at his English teacher with surprise. Only the big shots in school got to work on the McClymonds *Warrior*.

"Wow. Would I!" Morrie couldn't get any more words out. He just waited for Mr. Zeno to continue.

"You're a natural at sports. I know you run the quarter mile in track, that you've been in the Remar baseball league, and that you're in a lot of sandlot football. You go to all the games. Maybe you could write about some of them for the *Warrior*. We call it covering the story. And you could do drawings to go with the stories. How about it, Morrie?"

"Yes, sir." Morrie walked home feeling that his feet weren't even touching the ground. He felt like a kite with the string cut off. Morrie Turner writing for the school paper. Wait until Dad heard that!

"It means working harder at English," the teacher warned him. "You'll have to keep up your grades if you expect to work on the school paper. And you'll have to learn all kinds of writing, not just sentences to put in balloons over your comic characters."

Well, if words were part of it, Morrie would learn how to handle them, he decided. Just watch what he'd do next time Mr. Jenkins gave him a lesson for English class. He'd show him he could write, Morrie promised himself. He didn't have to wait long.

"You fellows will be looking for jobs when you get out of high school. Today let's see what kind of letter you could write to an employer. Try for something different," Mr. Zeno instructed, "something that would make him remember you as a person, as someone, not just a name at the bottom of a letter. All right, go ahead. I'll give you a half hour. See if you can sell yourself."

Questions from the students—"How do we begin?" "What do we have to tell him about ourselves?"—kept popping at Mr. Jenkins, but he only shook his head. Some of the boys started writing, but Morrie kept chewing on his pencil, thinking. He decided the others would probably all say "Dear Sir, I'm good in school. I work hard. I've never been in trouble. My family needs the dough."

If he were the man reading the letters, Morrie thought, he'd choose one that was different. He stopped chewing on his pencil and started thinking about people. He'd have to feel the same as the guy who was writing. What about a punch-drunk fighter who wanted to get out of the ring and get a real job, Morrie thought? Slowly his pencil started moving across the page.

"Dear Mister," he wrote. "How's about giving me a job? I've been knocked around a lot in and out of the boxing ring, and I got a lot of bounce. No job you could give me would be too hard to try. If I couldn't get it the first time, I'd bounce back for a second try. And I don't get tired easy. Just try me and I'll show you. It took three cents for this letter to come to you, but it'll take just a nickel phone call to bring me running to your door. I'm down right now, but ready to get up."

Morrie was so deep in his writing he hadn't noticed Mr. Jenkins standing at his elbow, reading over his shoulder. "You call that a letter?" he asked, his face red with anger. "Didn't you learn anything in class?"

"I was only trying to be different," Morrie answered.

"If you think that's satire, young man, leave it to someone with more skill than you. In the sports column of the newspaper you can write with color, with style, but when it comes to business—" Mr. Jenkins's face twitched. He crumpled the letter and threw it in the wastebasket.

Morrie felt like a friend was being thrown away. He had almost started to see in his mind a punch-drunk fighter trying to get on and maybe get a better job. And now Mr. Jenkins had tossed him in the wastebasket. Did everyone have to do things the same way, Morrie wondered?

Only that morning Morrie had seen a picture in *Esquire* magazine of "Esky," the little pop-eyed cartoon figure with the top hat and the monocle that everyone recognized at the newsstands. It was different. Nothing serious about that guy. And he was drawn by a black cartoonist, E. Sims Campbell. Morrie had read a story about him in the San Francisco newspapers. Campbell even drew harem girls in his panels.

Maybe he, Morrie, could draw something different some day, so that people looking at his characters would think of his name at the same time.

The three o'clock bell rang. Morrie slowly walked away from school by himself. Life was sure mixed up, he thought. How does a guy get to do what he wants to do?

Morrie hadn't even managed a byline on the school paper, his name over a story to show he had written it. He was sure his sports stories that were printed were as good as most of the others. But the white kids seemed to rate a byline easier. Was skin color really so important?

There was going to be a party tonight and Morrie didn't have time to be serious for long. He was taking a girl for the first time. He'd asked Letha, that slim, sparkly-eyed girl who never laughed at him at the wrong time. "Your drawing is great," she often told Morrie. They had met when he delivered the daily paper to her parents' home after school.

So what if he couldn't write the right kind of business letter or get a byline. Tonight he and Letha would walk to the party with Joe and his girlfriend, Rosa. They'd talk and laugh and have fun. Tomorrow he'd worry about whether he wanted to be a newspaperman or cartoonist or learn how to write proper letters. Not satire. He'd have to look up that word, Morrie thought.

Girls and words. He was getting all mixed up again. Morrie liked them both. Almost as well as drawing.

But girls, words, and drawing weren't Morrie's entire life. He was growing up. And growing up meant learning to fight, Morrie's brothers told him. Buster was good with his fists, and fought at the men-only smokers on Friday nights at the Yosemite Gym in West Oakland. Morrie played the drums in the band there, when dancing girls entertained.

Morrie started going there when he was only twelve, but big for his age, and the place fascinated him. John Henry Lewis, one-time light heavyweight champion of the world, had trained there, and his father owned the place. Even Max Baer, who was getting famous in the ring and the movies, came to Yosemite Gym.

It didn't take much coaxing to get Morrie to try putting on gloves against a bantamweight (one of the lighter classes of boxing) professional fighter who needed sparring partners. When Morrie put on shorts and boxing shoes and climbed into the ring, he thought it would be an easy way to make two dollars a round. The boxers just danced around and gave each other a poke now and then, Morrie thought.

But once inside the ropes, all Morrie could see were big gloves jabbing at his face. He couldn't "dance" fast enough to evade the blows at his nose, his eyes, his chin, his ribs, and his shoulders. After what seemed like hours of gloved fists battering away at him, the bell rang. Morrie swayed on his feet, gulping air into his lungs, trying to stand upright while the room was spinning.

Again the bell rang and someone pushed Morrie away from the protecting ropes. The battering gloves came right after him, and soon blood oozed from his nose. One eye was almost shut and the ring swam in circles. Morrie couldn't land even one punch against his opponent. Suddenly, as fists smashed into his head, his knees folded and hit the canvas, and the fight was over for Morrie before the second round ended.

That ended his fighting career, too. He never tried to get into the ring again. Anyway, he consoled himself, Mama didn't like to have her sons battering at people with their fists. "Too many people have chips on their shoulders," Mama warned against street fights. "Talk things over, like gentlemen."

Buster didn't agree. When a teacher at McClymonds High School called him a "dirty nigger," Buster knocked him flat. After that, he and his brothers were called "The Fighting Turners" at school.

Morrie's first day in gym class at McClymonds came after that. At roll call, when he answered to "Turner," the coach glared at him.

"Not another one of 'The Fighting Turners.' You'd better toe the line here, boy."

But trouble seemed to follow Morrie at high school. One day a friend "borrowed" some bicycles to ride to Technical High School to see a game. He asked Morrie and another boy to go along without telling them where he had gotten the bikes.

Riding three abreast down Thirty-eighth Street, the boys raced to see who could get to the neighboring high school first. When screeching police whistles followed them, Morrie and his friends stopped at the curb.

"Where do you think you kids are going?" bellowed a police officer. "Don't you know that riding three abreast is against the law? What are your names and where do you go to school?"

Bob, who had "borrowed" the bikes, tried to break away, but the officer grabbed him by the shoulder.

"All three of you, back to school, and we'll get to the bottom of this. Whose bikes are these, anyway?"

"We—we borrowed them," Morrie offered, suspecting the truth too late, and looking at Bob to finish the sentence.

"I swiped them, you nut," Bob whispered, "and now I'll have to go back to juvenile hall for sure."

"Keep still," Morrie motioned, "maybe you can get out of it."

Back at school in the principal's office, Bob shook his head and said nothing to all the questions the officer asked.

"One of them is a Turner kid. He's probably responsible," the principal told the policeman. Morrie knew if Bob told about stealing the bikes it would mean expulsion for his friend and he would be sent back to juvenile hall where there were bars on the window and awful food.

"I don't know whose bikes they are," Morrie kept telling the principal and the officer.

"Since the bikes are back, I'll suspend the boys for three days if you let them off this time," the principal said to the police officer.

There wasn't going to be another brush with the law, Morrie promised himself on the way home. He felt rotten about the whole thing, and he knew how mad Mom and Dad would would be at him. He'd get back to his drawing and stay out of trouble, Morrie vowed.

"The kid needs a fresh start," Dad decided when he heard the story. "And you stay out of trouble," he roared at Morrie.

That meant transferring from McClymonds to Berkeley High where nobody knew Morrie was one of "The Fighting Turners."

Morrie's graduation photo from Berkeley High School

Morrie drew cartoons for *Stars and Stripes* when he was in the service.

Chapter 4

A WORLD AT WAR

Pearl Harbor! On December 7, 1941, the Japanese attacked a United States Naval Base, Pearl Harbor, in Hawaii. The United States declared war on Japan and Germany and formally entered World War II.

Then "Dirty Japs" became part of almost everyone's vocabulary.

How could people change so quickly, look at former friends as enemies? Morrie wondered. A Japanese family who lived next door to the Turners was ordered to leave and to go to a relocation camp, a place where they and other Japanese-Americans would have no contact with other citizens. Morrie had liked them. They'd never been in trouble of any kind. They worked hard and kept their yard and home cleaner than any in the neighborhood. They lived quietly.

Morrie remembered all the kids in his neighborhood—black, yellow, brown, and white. Their color never did matter to him. They were all his friends. Like the Japanese family. And now, all of a sudden, people were looking at each other's skin.

Morrie felt he couldn't hate anyone, only the thought of people killing one another. Everyone was "getting into the war" and so was he. Morrie was graduated from Berkeley High School in 1942 and was drafted in February, 1943. But Morrie was sure it would be all over before he finished basic training. Like all the other fellows, Morrie wanted to be a pilot. That was the way to end the war fast.

"It's Lubbock, Texas for you," Morrie was told. Then later to Biloxi, Mississippi. That was where he would have precadet training to become a black pilot in the air force. Next would be Biloxi, Mississippi, where examinations to qualify were held.

What a break. Maybe he could go to New Orleans, Morrie thought, and visit his cousins and his aunt who lived in his dad's former home. Maybe he could even see the place where Mama taught school after she had graduated from Southern University.

On the train trip Morrie couldn't help remembering when

he was a kid and met his dad's train with his brothers. Dad still was a porter, but Morrie and he were on trains going in different directions now.

Stopping to visit his relatives in New Orleans, Morrie's first sight of the South was a sickening experience.

"You're black, you're black," the signs seemed to be shouting at him. He never really minded being black before, but now it seemed to imply that he was inferior. Water fountains, restrooms, waiting rooms, even theaters had signs by the door, "NO COLORED." In department stores there were separate drinking faucets for white and colored. Even bars had railing dividers.

Morrie met his young cousins, went to teenage dancing clubs with them; but he refused to go to segregated theaters. For kicks he rode with one of his cousins in a horse-drawn milk wagon that left milk bottles at customers' doors between two and three o'clock in the morning.

At home Morrie had known that racial differences existed. A friend, Phillips, one of the two best pitchers on the high school baseball team, didn't get a tryout with the Chicago White Sox because he was black. And of course, blacks didn't give speeches at junior high graduation exercises. Morrie knew that from experience.

But until now, prejudice had been something puzzling to

Morrie. He hadn't stopped to think much about it, because it hadn't happened too often. Now that he was here in the southern states, it was real. Blacks and whites were treated as different people. They lived in separate worlds.

In spite of everything, Morrie enjoyed meeting his kinfolks, and seeing their different way of life was an eye-opener.

And, in a corner of his mind, a new idea was planted. Maybe he, Morrie, with his drawings, could show that people are really alike and deserve to be treated the same. He didn't know what he could or would do, but he'd keep thinking about it, Morrie promised himself.

The days passed quickly. Morrie seemed to lose count of them. Living in his dream world, Mama would have said. He was having such a good time he didn't even think of the date he was due at Biloxi.

But the sealed orders he was carrying reminded him there was a war waiting to be fought.

"Where are your papers?" the guard roared, when Morrie finally reached the barracks at Biloxi after a train trip. He was only a few days late.

Ripping open the sealed packet Morrie gave him, the guard snorted, "You were due here three days ago. Don't you know you could get court-martialed for being AWOL? And that means 'Away Without Official Leave,' in case you don't know."

How could he tell them he forgot the date because so much was happening on this memorable trip? Morrie decided he'd better keep his mouth shut.

How the mess was untangled, Morrie was too ashamed to question and too tired to try to keep up with the officers' efforts to place him. No outfit had any record of Morrie's assignment, and they shuffled him from one place to another, but he didn't seem to be listed anywhere. All he wanted was a place to sleep. When finally he was told to stretch out on the crowded barracks floor, even that was welcome.

"You get a three-day testing program to see if you fly or what you do," Morrie was told the next day. "Some pass, some fail, some get another job. That's the way it goes, kid," the sergeant told him kindly. "Just wait, you'll find out."

It wasn't good news. Morrie found that he was washed out after the third day of testing.

For a guy who had never been away from home, things happened fast now that Morrie was in uniform.

He was shipped to Shreveport, Louisiana, for military police training. Then Morrie rejoined the 477th All-Black Bomber Division as part of the ground personnel, in military police, at Goodman Air Force Base in Kentucky.

"It's guard duty for you, Turner," Morrie was told on his first orders. It meant marching back and forth past the garbage dump, hour after hour.

"You call this war?" Morrie muttered to himself as he marched between swarms of flies and the sickening stench of decaying food. What was he supposed to "protect," Morrie wondered. His shoulders were sore from trying to hold them in a straight line, his feet ached, and his nose felt pinched from trying to hold his breath to keep out the sour odor.

The minute hand on Morrie's wristwatch hardly seemed to move after miles and miles of marching. Morrie could hardly keep his eyes open. He decided to sit down for a minute. The next thing he knew someone was shaking him and an angry white face was pushing into Morrie's.

"Asleep on duty! That means the guardhouse for you. You're under arrest." An officer pushed Morrie into a small cavelike cell. Bars and bunk beds were all he could see as the door clanked shut behind him. Morrie felt too miserable now to care about sleeping.

"I was going to fight for my country, and here I am under arrest for falling asleep," Morrie moaned. "Just like a kid. How do I fight a war from here?"

There was a war waging in the Pacific and in Europe, but Morrie was sitting in a cell in the United States.

Morrie learned there was to be a hearing at his base. He wondered if he'd have to face a firing squad or what.

"Relax, relax," his defense attorney told Morrie. "You're not the first guy to fall alseep on duty. Everything will be all right. Morrie was found not guilty and urged to make a clean start.

"I've landed a job in special services for you, right here in Kentucky," the captain told Morrie. "What can you do best?"

"Draw," Morrie muttered, his eyes down. Kid stuff, he thought and here I'm in a man's war.

"Say, that's not bad. Maybe you can get on the *Stars and Stripes*. You know how famous it is. It was begun during the Civil War, was printed again during World War I, and started again during this war. It gives daily on-the-scene news, not only to soldiers, but to every other paper and press service in the world."

Morrie had heard about the *Stars and Stripes*. Staff members were in the front lines, jumped with paratroopers, sometimes became prisoners of war, or were among those killed in action. *Stars and Stripes* always put the soldier first, and gave equal importance to a general and a private. It was GI Joe's link with what was happening on the fighting front and at home, Morrie had learned. *Stars and Stripes* ranked tops in American newspaper history; its staff

51

included many great journalists such as Alexander Wolcott, Harold Ross, Ernie Pyle, Bud Hotton, Andy Rooney, and others. Cartoonist Bill Mauldin and John Fischetti were also published in *Stars and Stripes*.

"Colonel Benjamin Davis of West Point believes in giving every black man a chance," Morrie was told. (Davis was one of the first blacks to graduate from West Point.) "He expects the best from every man."

Now Morrie didn't mind the early bugle call, the drilling, or even the mess hall food. For the first time in his life he was with other people who had similar goals. Some of the *Stars and Stripes* staff had been well known in civilian life. If he lived to be a hundred years old, Morrie thought, he'd never forget the day he met Greeley Hall, who had been a newspaperman even before the war. He was an important cog in this all-black division. Hall, a black cartoonist, was noted for his work in black publications in Little Rock, Arkansas.

"Learn how to do your thing better than anyone else," Hall told Morrie. "We'll teach you what we can. But take it easy. You don't have to run the Olympics on the drawing board."

Morrie's only drawing lessons had been when he'd seen Bill Holman drawing "Smokey Stover" in a movie. He thought that all cartoonists actually drew at a fast rate of speed. So Morrie had gotten into the habit of working with lightning strokes.

"Slow down, kid. You have a lot to learn. Drawing is slow, step-by-step. You have to think fast, get an idea. Visualize it as a picture. Then tighten it to tell the story in balloons over your characters. And then draw your figures," Hall told him. "Now watch us."

Morrie's eyes became blotters, trying to absorb everything he saw Hall and the other experienced man on the newspaper staff do.

Trying to slow down his pace, he thought about a character he could create. It had to be something he could call his own. What did he know best? A bumbling black, like himself, who seemed to have a talent for doing everything wrong. "I'll call him 'Rail Head,'" Morrie decided, "because he has such a thick skull he always has to do everything wrong before he can find the right way."

Working at his drawing board one rainy day, Morrie didn't see Hall watching him draw "Rail Head." "You've made him more likeable than dumb. I think he'll be okay. How would you like to polish him up for the next issue?"

When the newspaper was published, Morrie hurried through the pages to find his strip with "Rail Head." He smelled the fresh ink. He felt giddy, as if he had swallowed a bottle of booze in one gulp. This was the kind of joy of accomplishment he'd never known before.

"Well how do you like your cartoon in print?" Hall asked. "It's pretty good," he added. "You'll be right up with the pros soon. But don't forget, Morrie," Hall warned, "there's another edition coming.

"Start right now thinking about what 'Rail Head' is going to do next. You'll be getting fans. They'll want to see this character in trouble. That's great. It makes the men feel like better soldiers when they see somebody bumbling orders."

"I'll sure keep him going, even if I have to stay awake nights figuring it out," Morrie promised.

"Only don't fall asleep at the drawing board. You might not get off as easily a second time," Hall laughed. "Come in and join the staff in a bull session. We're going to plan some things. Remember, there's a war on and we have to keep up the guys' morale with laughs. That's part of our job."

Morrie didn't think he would be asked to tap dance in a comedy act, "Bugs and the Big Time Trip," but that's what he was handed as an assignment for the big variety show the following Saturday night. "All you have to do is keep time and bow once in a while. 'Flash' is what actors call it. You'll be funny enough stumbling through your routine to make the guys laugh, and that's what we want."

One never knew what Special Services meant, Morrie discovered.

The chaplain came to him one day and asked Morrie, "What do you know about women?"

"Like what?" Morrie wanted to know.

"Older women," the chaplain smiled. "I want a picture of one for the Mother's Day cover of the chapel bulletin. Think you can draw one?"

That was easy. Morrie took a snapshot of his mother out of his pocket, although he really didn't have to look at it to remember the smiling round face, her sparkling eyes, and her now-graying hair. When the bulletin with her picture on the cover was printed, Morrie sent her a copy.

"Doing something for church, that's good, Son," she wrote him promptly.

Morrie had to admit it made him feel good, too. Maybe after the war he could do something that wasn't just for laughs.

Morrie and Letha not long after their marriage

Chapter 5

FREE LANCER

Although he stayed in the United States, Morrie felt as much a part of the war as the servicemen overseas.

"The medics give GIs blood plasma, the mess halls provide food, but you fellows give them belly laughs. And when a guy laughs, he wants to live," Greeley Hall told the staff. Listening to every word, Morrie felt Hall was talking especially to him.

Morrie told Letha about Hall in his letters to her in Berkeley. She was still in high school and working part-time in the post office. Whenever the newspaper staff went to the commissary for a hamburger or a Coke, and the talk turned to girls, Morrie could always imagine seeing Letha.

"It's like going to college, learning from these guys who

have been working on big newspapers," he wrote to her.

When the jukeboxes wailed out popular songs, Morrie always thought of Letha. Billy Eckstine's voice and all the other popular singers could be heard. "I'll be seeing you, in all the old familiar places" rang through the barracks as loud as six different radios could blare. Whoever sang the song, it was Letha that Morrie saw. He kept remembering their walks around Berkeley together. Or the baseball games they had seen. He longed to see her again.

When the fighting in the Pacific ended on August 14, 1945, Morrie knew it would be only a matter of time until he was a civilian again. He couldn't wait to get back to California. Settling down, having a home of his own to share with Letha—if she would marry him—became the most important thing in Morrie's life.

On his return to Berkeley, the first thing Morrie did after he saw his family was to visit Letha.

"Will you, will you, will you?" he stammered, forgetting the beautiful words he had rehearsed in his mind when he planned asking her to marry him. Then they were in each others' arms. He must have found the right words. They went to both parents to tell them they were going to be married.

Soon after their wedding, they were in their own apartment.

"You made the first big step toward a career while you were in the service," Letha told Morrie one night when they were talking about their future. "From here on, it's up to you what you want to be."

"It's got to be cartooning, baby, I'll have to make it on my own now, or forget it," Morrie told her, banging his fists on the table so that the coffee mugs jumped.

"Who's fighting you? I'm with you. But there's a lot more to learn, now that you don't have the pros at your elbow for advice," Letha reminded Morrie.

"Meanwhile we've got to eat," Morrie frowned. "I'll keep up that correspondence course on cartooning that I started before I went into the service. And I'll try for a job at the police department. They advertised for a clerk. I even did some typing and office work part of the time in Special Services. I should be able to handle it."

When he saw the number of servicemen and other applicants who took the test, Morrie wasn't sure.

"All right, fellows," the examiner told the roomful of men after they filled out the required forms. "We'll let you know by mail how you rated."

While he waited, Morrie crammed the days and nights with drawing and study. For the first time he learned about marketing cartoons.

"You don't just draw them, you have to find someone to buy them. Someone who'll use them in a magazine or newspaper," he told Letha, who always listened. She wanted to know more about this new work Morrie was trying.

"Right now you just think about keeping well and giving me a son," Morrie teased. Letha had told him that by the next year there would be a baby in their family.

"So it's up to me to make the dough to pay the butcher, the grocer, and the doctor bill," Morrie reminded Letha.

When the news came that he'd passed the test for the police department, Morrie and Letha danced like kids. "Out for dinner tonight, we celebrate," Morrie decided. "Then to work tomorrow."

When he left for work the next morning, Morrie took a lesson from the correspondence course with him.

"Why that?" Letha wanted to know. "You have to give the police department your full time, if you want to keep the job."

"Sure, I know. I intend to, honey. But there's lunch and break time. And I don't want to waste any of it."

Typing police reports and citizen complaints kept Morrie busy. It was bad enough to deal with adults getting in trouble, but making out records for kids stealing and traveling in gangs bothered Morrie.

Nights, while Letha was knitting and making baby clothes, Morrie worked at his drawing.

"I've got an idea, a cartoon for *Baker's Helper* magazine," Morrie told Letha one night. "All the trade journals, the magazines published by different businesses, want cartoons. But many of them can't pay to have a regular artist on their staff, so they buy from free lancers. And that, baby, is me." Morrie pointed in a wide circle to himself, his drawing board, and the living room cluttered with old newspapers, opened magazines, and rough drafts of comic strips.

The baby, Morrie, Jr., and his first free-lance check arrived in 1947, and Letha pretended she didn't know which pleased Morrie more.

"This kid, he's forever. That five-dollar check from the *Baker's Helper* went for the baby's milk already," Morrie told her. "Remember I'm a father now, the head of a family. I've got more reasons than ever to want to make good as a cartoonist."

Now the evening circle included three. First it was little Morrie in his playpen. Then little Morrie was crawling around the room, or walking and getting into everything. But Letha always was careful to see that Morrie had drawing time at night after work, even with Morrie, Jr., wanting his Dad's time and attention.

Morrie listened to Letha's ideas. She had some good ideas and as time went on some of them turned into checks for cartoons she suggested. Money came from such well-known magazines as *Better Homes & Gardens, True, Argosy, Extension,* and *Negro Digest.* Time passed quickly for Morrie, working for the police department and doing more and more cartoons.

"When we hit the $300 mark for cartoon sales in one month, I'm going to quit the police department," Morrie told Letha in 1964. I've been with them for eleven years now, and it's time to make a break. We've got some government bonds. You're a good manager.

"I'll take what's in my retirement fund and cash it, and we'll sink it all into an offset printing press and work from home. We can make Christmas cards, letterheads, invitations, calendars, and church bulletins. You can be business manager. And Morrie, Jr., can be on the eating-the-profits end. But we'll make it. What do you say, Letha?"

When he told his family about his decision to go into business for himself, his grandmother groaned.

"Just because Morrie sells a few drawings, he goes off his nut. Gives up a good steady job to knock himself out in a business that might not make any money."

As long as Letha didn't think he was nuts, Morrie didn't

care. He wasn't a kid any longer. He was a husband, a father, and a cartoonist. And now a businessman. He'd show Dad and his brothers that he could make a living with his scribbling. Morrie Turner, free lancer. He liked the sound of it.

Chapter 6

"WEE PALS"

After he decided to devote full time to drawing, Morrie's work slowly started to shape into a paying occupation.

In 1963 when he went to the Northern California Cartoonists and Gag Writers meeting in San Francisco, he was the only black member. But men of his race were making it in the limelight, like Dick Gregory, the black comedian and political satirist whom Morrie met the same year.

By then Morrie had finished his first comic strip, "Dinky Fellas," which he sold to black publications. *The Berkeley* (California) *Post*, a weekly, started using it first, then *The Chicago Daily Defender* bought it.

Morrie found that his best work was drawing kids.

"Dinky Fellas," with its all-black characters, was running

five days a week in *The Chicago Daily Defender*, and readers liked the strip. But Morrie wasn't satisfied.

He really wanted to do a comic strip with kids of all races and nationalities like the ones he grew up with in West Oakland. Morrie wanted to draw white, brown, yellow, and black kids playing, fighting, and disagreeing, but still remaining friends.

But most publishers didn't think the public was ready to accept an integrated strip. People hadn't learned to live like that yet, Morrie was told. That made Morrie more determined than ever to keep working on his idea. Maybe kids could teach grown-ups how to accept all races as friends.

Meanwhile Morrie kept working on his new strip, which finally replaced "Dinky Fellas." He christened it "Wee Pals," representing kids of all races and nationalities.

Nipper, a black boy wearing a Confederate cap, became his main character. Morrie felt he could remember his own days as a kid to make Nipper real.

Oliver would be the name of Nipper's white friend who was a brain and didn't mind letting everyone know about it.

Randy, another black, would be different from Nipper, carrying the NAACP (National Association for the Advancement of Colored People) banner, which meant to him, "Never Abandon an Adolescent Caucasian Pal."

Morrie then added George, an Oriental, who always wore a soft cap and could quote Confucius when the kids needed advice.

For a truly native American, Morrie added Rocky, an Indian who is color-blind when it comes to choosing friends and having playmates of all kinds.

Then there was Paul, the Mexican-American kid.

Wellington, the inquisitive one with his hair in his eyes, would always ask the others questions.

Later Morrie added Jerry, honoring a special Jewish friend.

But it couldn't be a strip with just male characters because Morrie wanted girls to read it too. So in came blond, white Connie, an independent two-fisted fighter who did everything stereotyped girls aren't supposed to do. And black Sibyl added more of the female viewpoint to the action.

With this mixture, Morrie felt his kids would have something to say to everyone, in spite of their different skins, homes, churches, and ways of thinking. Keeping that bunch together, something was bound to happen every day.

Although he was convinced his characters could show children and adults how to live together peacefully, syndicates that sold comic strips to newspapers weren't eager to buy "Wee Pals." They wanted sure sellers and didn't want to gamble on something that they granted was "a swell idea" but weren't certain their readers would accept. That's what publishers kept telling Morrie.

As he had done before in his life whenever he was stuck, Morrie decided to take over the action himself. Letha provided the answer. Why not self-syndicate, she suggested? Letha was working now, in the Social Security office in San Francisco, and even if "Wee Pals" sales were slow at first, her paychecks would keep them in groceries.

"It's a great idea. I like what you're trying to show; people learning to get along peaceably and laughing together. Keep right on trying and 'Wee Pals' will be read all over the country if you just give it some time," Letha encouraged.

This meant writing business letters to newspapers. Morrie cringed, remembering his high school English assignment. He'd have to get ideas to keep "Wee Pals" in action and saying something different every day. Then draw the strips. Then sell them.

The ideas and the drawing were like being in heaven for Morrie. But he dreaded the job of selling the strip. He wished it could just miraculously appear in print.

But many letters went out, and while newspaper editors sent encouraging replies, they didn't buy the strip. Then

Morrie sent it to syndicates and the same thing happened. Morrie was beginning to think it was time to forget about drawing and get a regular job. Then, Lew Little, a syndicate representative from San Francisco, who heard of "Wee Pals" through *The Berkeley Gazette* editor, came to Morrie. "I'll buy it and sell it," Lew said. And that's what happened. So in 1964 "Wee Pals" was finally syndicated.

Then Morrie's name began to be recognized throughout the country. He even received fan mail. Many people didn't know he was black.

"What I want to know," a man from Detroit wrote, "is . . . do you really know any black people?"

"Only my mother and father, my wife, and my son," Morrie replied to him. Morrie always answered fan letters. He was glad to hear from new friends.

Soon newspapers in other countries were buying his strip.

"Do all American kids sell lemonade?" a boy from Zambia, in Africa, wrote when "Wee Pals" reached his country.

"That proves I've got to be extra careful in everything I show the kids saying and doing," Morrie told Letha when they were discussing "Wee Pals."

Morrie wasn't the only one now thinking that people of all races, colors, and nationalities should know each other better. If Americans and other nationalities and races are to live peacefully, they must understand each other, more and more editors were saying in their newspaper columns. And more schools were teaching the same idea.

Every month more and more newspapers kept asking for Morrie's integrated strip.

Since they signed the syndicate contract, Morrie and Letha were business as well as marriage partners, working together. Now Morrie was free to work on ideas and drawings. Selling the strip would be handled for him, with his earnings going up as more newspapers used "Wee Pals." It meant that Morrie had "arrived" as a cartoonist and writer.

"Tonight we celebrate," Letha told him. Her family arranged a party for them to celebrate the syndicate contract and to tell Morrie how proud they were of him. Even Mama, who always said liquor was something she could do without, had her first taste of champagne when everyone drank a toast to Morrie and long life to his "Wee Pals."

While shopping with Letha one day, Morrie almost stumbled over two kids lying flat on their stomachs on the floor of the supermarket, busy with crayons and a coloring book. The boy and girl, about kindergarten age, could have been on a desert island. They were so busy they didn't notice anyone around them.

When he was their age he loved to color and draw, too, Morrie remembered. Instead of checking his shopping list, Morrie came to a dead halt, rubbing his chin with his thumb.

"It doesn't look as if you're thinking about groceries. What's on your mind now?" Letha wanted to know, taking the shopping list from Morrie.

"I've got an idea."

"Another one?" Letha laughed. "Can it wait until after dinner?"

They had hardly finished eating that night when Morrie started. "About that idea today. I was just thinking. When I go to schools with my chalk talks and draw 'Wee Pals' for the kids, I'm surprised how few of the blacks or whites know anything about the contribution black people have made to this country. Maybe if I did a coloring book about them, kids could learn the easy way about famous blacks. Letha, you could do the research. I'm thinking about a book with 'Wee Pals' characters talking about famous blacks, and then a picture page of the person for the readers to color."

"You could use Mary Bethune, George Washington Carver, and Frederick Douglass," Letha suggested.

"That's a good start. But what about lesser-known people, like actor Ira Aldridge or Dr. Charles Drew, who found a way of keeping blood plasma? And there's Bill Pickett, the black cowboy with the Lewis and Clark expedition," Morrie added.

"I think you've got something good," Letha agreed. "I'll go to the library tomorrow and dig through the book *Famous Negro Americans* and see how many I can find who did different things that kids would like to know about."

That was the start of the large *Black and White Coloring Book* that was published in 1969 during Negro History Week.

Deciding whom to include and whom to leave out was the hardest part for Morrie. He began the storytelling coloring book with Crispus Attucks, the first black man to die in the American Revolution, who was killed in the Boston Massacre, March 5, 1770.

Then there was Benjamin Banneker, inventor, mathematician, and astronomer. Jean Baptist Point Du Sable, founder of a trading post in the city that became Chicago, was next. Sojourner Truth, first black woman orator, who fought for abolition and women's suffrage, was discussed in another section. Frederick Douglass, lecturer and traveler, who was a slave until he was twenty-one and then became a freedom seeker and later United States minister to Haiti, deserved space too, Morrie decided.

Kids that Morrie questioned didn't know about Ira Aldridge, a leading Shakespearean actor who lived in the early 1880s, so pages were allotted to him. Next was a picture story of Hiram Revels of Mississippi, the first black senator. The minibiographies continued, with Matthew Henson, scientist and explorer who went to the North Pole, and W.E.B. DuBois, a professor at Atlanta University who became the editor-in-chief of the *Encyclopedia Africana*.

In the coloring book, "Wee Pals" taught about Bill Pickett, famous cowboy, who was known as "The Dusty Demon from Texas." The kids discussed what everyone should know about George Washington Carver, scientist and inventor, and Mary McLeod Bethune, early educator.

Morrie hoped it would be fun for all kids, discovering new friends in the *Black and White Coloring Book* and learning about people who lived before they were born. Among his favorites was Dr. Charles Drew, whose plasma research saved thousands of lives during World War II.

Other better-known people in the book included W.C. Handy, noted musician called the "Father of the Blues," and Langston Hughes, writer and novelist whose books are in school libraries.

The *Black and White Coloring Book* was important to Morrie because he wanted to share his pride in black people.

It also gave Letha her first byline in the book for her help in research. With this, she began publicly sharing her husband's work as partner in an important team.

After finishing the coloring book, Morrie decided to let "Wee Pals" carry his message further. He included miniature biographies of famous Negroes, Indians, Jews, Orientals, and Mexican-Americans in a panel for the "Wee Pals" Sunday comic strips that went into thousands of homes.

The *Black and White Coloring Book* and its little biographies tell stories that were never in school history books, teacher friends told Morrie. Kids liked it, too, because they found they could do history homework by reading "Wee Pals."

The strip was seven years old by now, and the next step was to put "Wee Pals" in a paperback book that was printed in 1969. Then, *Nipper's Secret Power* became a hardback book in 1970.

Meanwhile, Morrie continued visiting schools as often as his busy schedule would allow. While doing chalk talks for boys and girls, he asked them about their own ideas for books.

"What do you think freedom is?" Morrie asked a class to keep the kids talking while he drew sketches of them and "Wee Pals" to give to them.

"Freedom is holding hands with anyone you want." "Freedom is the right to be wrong." "Freedom is singing when you feel good." To dozens of kids, freedom meant dozens of different things. Again it sparked an idea in Morrie.

He asked hundreds of children their answer to the question, and the best ones were brought to life by "Wee Pals" characters in cartoons that became a paperback book *Freedom Is. . . .* Other books that followed were *God Is Groovy*, printed in 1972; *Wee Pals (Kid Power) Welcome to the Club* made its debut in 1978; and *All God's Chillun Got Soul*, featuring the Wee Pals Kid Power Gang, followed in 1980.

Freedom Is. . . left its imprint on Morrie. To him freedom meant drawing, even though people had said when he was a boy, "Too bad he's colored." It meant giving black people credit for their deeds, and looking for new ways to teach kids of all colors how to get along with each other. It meant doing television commercials that showed kids good eating habits so they could learn about nutrition and have stronger, healthier bodies.

It even meant having life-sized figures of "Wee Pals" on the state capitol grounds in Sacramento, California.

"Now my kids are really on the scene," Morrie thought. But having them in the homes of all kinds of people, through his newspaper columns and books, was even more satisfying.

Letha and Morrie, Jr.

Chapter 7

A TIME FOR GIVING

Even when he went to bed at night, Morrie couldn't get "Wee Pals" off his mind. "I've gotta get at least three good ideas a day to keep them going," he told Letha. "When a thought hits me, I've got to put it down."

Morrie always had a pencil and pad in his pocket. He even kept one under his bed. If he woke up at night with a situation for a strip in his mind, he wrote a short note to remind himself how to enlarge it later.

"Enough is enough," Letha stormed at home one night when the light went on for the third time. "If you can do without sleep, I can't. I don't complain about what you do in the daytime. And I'm willing to help all the day, but nights, people need *some* rest."

When Letha spoke that way, Morrie didn't argue.

"All right, honey, all right. No more lights on when you're sleeping."

But Morrie didn't promise no more note writing. When he woke up after that, he would slowly slither out of bed, reach for the pad on the floor, and scrawl a note in the dark.

"Anything to keep peace," he told Letha one morning when she found the notepad under the bed before he had a chance to put in on his desk.

If Letha woke up after that, she pretended to be asleep. After all, Morrie had to keep his ideas perking day and night, she knew by now. Their home on Lorina Street in Berkeley changed into a workshop with drawing board, typewriters, and newspaper clippings cluttering every room.

Meanwhile the world was not peaceful, and servicemen of all ages were again going to war zones.

The Vietnam headlines gnawed at Morrie as he read the front-page news before turning to see what other cartoonists were producing in comics and satire (he knew what the word meant now).

"I wish I could do something to make the fighting end," Morrie kept telling Letha. But he found wishing wouldn't end it.

One day a letter from the National Cartoonists Society

showed him how he could help fellows in the combat zones.

"We would like you to be one of six American cartoonists going to entertain the troops in Vietnam," the letter he received in November of 1967 informed him.

It would mean twenty-seven days near the battle lines, talking to soldiers, kidding them till they laughed, drawing cartoons of the men and of "Wee Pals" to give to the boys in uniform, and giving them a fast line of chatter to keep their minds off their danger and their pain.

"Will you go?" Letha asked.

Would he! If the USO (United Service Organization) and National Cartoonists Society felt having him at hospitals and near the fighting lines would help, that was enough.

"Darn right I'll go," Morrie told his family.

"It'll mean drawing a month's supply of comics in advance. No production while you're overseas. And danger from enemy planes and guns," Letha reminded him with a worried look.

"We can do it, babe," Morrie told Letha.

They were a team. She was working full time with him now, doing his research, writing letters, keeping notes, reminding Morrie when his strips were due at publishers. It would mean that Letha would have to work at double speed, too, before he left.

But Letha felt the same way Morrie did. It would give her a chance to show she cared about what was happening in Vietnam. Her bit would be to help him to be able to go.

Morrie's mother proudly accompanied Letha to the San Francisco airport the day he left. He was to meet other cartoonists there. He only knew Jack Tippit, a famous magazine cartoonist, who was to be the trip supervisor.

Morrie was as pleased as a kid to see the outstretched hands of welcome waiting for him. There was Bil Keane of "The Family Circus" and "Channel Chuckles" strips. Bill Saunders, an editorial cartoonist from *The Milwaukee Journal* was next. Then Willard Mullins, the great sports cartoonist whom Morrie had admired and studied when he was a kid, and Howard Schneider who drew "Eek and Meek."

As the plane took off, Morrie's stomach seemed to jump into his throat. This was his first jet trip. As the plane lifted into the sky, Morrie wasn't sure if he was nervous about the flight or worried about what was ahead. But he sure didn't care about flying. He wondered if his hands would ever get steady enough to draw for anyone.

After seventeen hours of flying, Morrie and the other cartoonists were given regular fighting gear to wear—jackets, pants, boots, and fatigue caps, but no guns. Their pencils, pens, brushes, and chalk were their ammunition.

On his first hospital inspection tour at Saigon (now Ho Chi Minh City), Morrie saw kids young enough to be his son, Morrie, Jr., with parts of their bodies blown off. Some were blind. Some were in wheelchairs. Morrie wondered if he could do anything to bring a smile to their pain-etched faces.

Meanwhile his own stomach was in knots. Morrie, Jr., was in the navy, "somewhere overseas." Each time a litter of wounded men came in, Morrie prayed more fervently than he ever had in his life, "Don't let it be my son."

But he kept making his rounds at the hospital, drawing caricatures of the patients. The welcome they gave him made Morrie forget his jumping stomach and his shaking hands. For the first time he was truly grateful that "Wee Pals" was now in newspapers all over the United States and other countries as well. The servicemen knew his "Wee Pals." They were their friends. And they needed so much to have something to laugh about.

"Oh God, let them return home to laugh with their families," Morrie found himself praying inwardly behind the smile that became his mask as he worked. Would Mama love this. He, Morrie, praying, when he hadn't been to church in—he didn't remember when.

The days passed quickly, with jeeps, bombs, and gunfire in the background as the cartoonists took sixteen different flights in South Vietnam to reach more men. They visited the First and Third Marine Divisions. They went to hospitals, camps, recreation centers, and the enlisted men's clubs and drew more than three thousand caricatures of the servicemen they met.

Through it all Morrie felt as if it must be a dream. But helicopters bringing in wounded men made him know it was real. How many of them had he drawn for, and laughed with, the day before?

When Morrie dropped in his bunk at night, dead tired, he no longer felt under the bed for a pad on which to write comic ideas. He knew now he had to do something serious and, he hoped, good. He wanted to show how he felt about these young people who were giving so much in the hope that the world would be safer for everyone. The killings just mustn't go on, Morrie kept telling himself. But what can a little guy like me do to stop it? He wondered.

Each night for the twenty-seven days he was in Vietnam, Morrie wrote his feelings to Letha. This was later published as "Cartoonist in Vietnam," in St. Joseph's Messenger.

Finally the day came to return home. Morrie no longer had to keep the gay chatter Ping-Ponging out of his mouth, his chalk flying as he talked. With Letha he could, without shame, let the long held-back tears flow.

"Those guys gave me more than I ever gave them," Morrie told his wife. "They made me see so many things differently. Each of us has to have a purpose in life. I hope with my drawings, and maybe some writing, to give something. I want to be a citizen of the world, not just the U.S.A."

The answer came through at his drawing board while Morrie kept on working on his "Wee Pals," aiming first to give a chuckle or a grin to his readers, but leaving behind a message of goodwill.

The National Conference of Christians and Jews presented him with their Brotherhood Award. B'nai B'rith Anti-Defamation League of Philadelphia chose him for its humanitarian award of 1968-69. He was presented with the Northern California Award of Merit during Negro History Week in 1969. The list kept growing and Morrie kept working.

And it all started out with a little black kid like himself, Morrie marveled.

But it wouldn't stop here. Morrie had other ideas. Maybe he could teach kids to be proud of their race, his black race, make them want to give of their ability and talent to others.

After he had a little rest, after the war scenes grew dimmer in his memory, he and Letha would figure out something else to do. He'd start. Tomorrow.

Morrie was bone weary that spring day in 1969. He'd been trying to keep his promise to himself to "do something." Now it seemed he never stopped working.

"I feel I could use a dozen more hands to do all the things that I need to do," Morrie told Letha. "I have to draw a month's supply of 'Wee Pals' strips for the syndicate. And some publishers want to talk to me about doing cartoons for twenty-four books for kids who are poor readers.

"Then I promised to work with the Berkeley Public Library 'Wee Pals' Summer Reading Program to see if we can keep kids reading during summer vacation. Five hundred already have signed up to attend."

Everywhere he went, someone asked Morrie to draw cartoons. So he decided the best thing to do would be to teach a class for people who liked drawing best, just as he did.

"Maybe you should have been twins," Letha kidded. "Then you could do twice as many things."

"Let's see what today's mail brings," Morrie told Letha as he rolled up his sleeves to start the day's work at the drawing board.

Letha shuffled through a handful of envelopes. "This one's from Washington, D.C. I wonder who it's from?"

As he opened the envelope, Morrie puckered his lips in a low whistle.

"What do you know about that!" he shouted, jumping to his feet. "It's asking me to be on the White House Conference on Children. And that's not all," Morrie gasped. "They want me to serve as vice chairman of the Child Development and Mass Media Section.

"Wow, look who else is on it. I'm to be cochairman with Fred Rogers of the 'Mister Rogers' TV show. And Joan Cooney of 'Sesame Street' will be working with us, too. And their editors and writers."

"But what are you supposed to do?" Letha wanted to know.

"Part of it is to help decide what kinds of programs are good for kids to watch on TV," Morrie told Letha as he scanned the papers. Morrie was pacing back and forth now, mopping beads of perspiration from his forehead.

"Me, Morrie Turner, to the White House."

"That's the conference that President Theodore Roosevelt started in 1909, that Booker T. Washington served on," Letha said in a whisper, glad of the research she had done for Morrie. "I remember, it's held only once every ten years, and some of the most important people in the country have served on it," she added, her eyes shining with pride. "It's too bad you're so busy and haven't time to do anything more," Letha told Morrie.

"I'm not too busy for this. I'll make the time, even if I have to stay up night and day to clear up the other work."

The days that followed didn't seem to have enough hours.

Morrie learned, in other letters, that he had been chosen "for your work on brotherhood of children of all races. We're seeking positive ways to answer the needs of children . . . to provide opportunities for every child."

That sounded so important that even at night when he should have been sleeping, Morrie was jotting down ideas. And Letha even turned on the light so he could see better.

"We want ways to help every child to learn to read . . . to reduce the 25 percent who can't now," his instructions told Morrie.

Finally the day came when Morrie was due to board the plane going to Washington, D.C. His stomach jumped into his throat again, as he waved good-bye to Letha. It wasn't fear of a plane crash. It was because he was so excited to be part of this big job.

As he watched the dome of the capitol come in view, when the plane circled before landing, Morrie's heart beat faster than it ever had when he was running track. At last the day is here when the color of a person's skin doesn't matter, Morrie thought. It is what is in his heart and mind and how he uses his God-given talent.

"Please help me," Morrie prayed as fervently as his

mother could ever have asked. "Help me to do a good job. Something that will help all kids so that their tomorrows will be better."

Morrie left the plane with a briefcase in his hand, a song in his heart, his fingers clutching a pencil, ready to start.

He was heading for the White House to help give ideas to make reading and television more fun and a better way of learning for all kids in the United States. Each of them— those masses of children in different places throughout the country—were like flesh and blood "Wee Pals."

They would be the "Rainbow Power" of the future, Morrie knew.

Morrie listens to Mary Beth, a daughter of one of his friends, as his granddaughter Nicole and grandsons Morrie III and Nathan look on.

Chapter 8

NOW A TEACHER WITH A NAME OF HIS OWN

After he returned from Washington, Morrie was ready to plunge back into his cartooning. He hoped some of the recommendations made by his section of the White House Conference on Children would become TV fare for kids. The suggestions were for less violence and more educational themes, presented in an enjoyable way.

"Would you be a guest speaker at my art class at Laney Trade School?" a teacher he had never met asked Morrie in a telephone call one day. "Everyone wants to know about cartooning and you're just the right person to give us the know-how from your experience."

By this time Morrie was accustomed to talking to all kinds of groups of different ages.

"I guess I'll have to cancel any other appointments you have for that day," Letha smiled at Morrie. She knew he'd do anything to encourage others to try the work he enjoyed so much.

Morrie prepared a speech for the class, but when he got there, the young men and women and older students, too, kept interrupting, "Draw for us, Morrie. Draw for us."

With the chalk gripped between his thumb and second finger, Morrie drew and talked at the same time.

"How do you sell?" "Who buys the stuff?" "How much money do you make?" Questions kept popping at Morrie from all over the room, and the period ended before he could give all the answers. The class members crowded around him. They wouldn't leave. When it was time to close the building, hoarse and happy, Morrie started packing his things.

"You know," the teacher told him, "I didn't realize there was so much to cartooning. You could give a separate course on that subject alone, from the interest shown here today."

But in spite of all his experience, credentials were necessary to teach, Morrie discovered. Into his crowded schedule he squeezed classes at the University of California so he could be eligible.

In 1970, at the age of 47, Morrie started teaching cartooning at Laney Community College, four hours each Monday night for twenty-eight weeks. Now he was a real teacher, with a gold-sealed credential from the state of California.

"A laughing class," the other teachers in the building called it, because of the happy sounds from the room.

"You can't be serious teaching humor," Morrie defended himself. For instance, he'd tell the class to draw a picture of a cop who stopped them for speeding. Or they'd discuss a joke.

With a cup of coffee in his hand, a ready word of encouragement, and quick praise for effort, Morrie found his students were producing good work. Most of them had daytime jobs, but still came to his night classes.

Bob Shoen, who was majoring in optometry, admitted he came to the class to develop a sense of humor. An Oriental student started selling the comic strip he created to a Chinese newspaper.

But one woman, who said there was too much laughing in the class, dropped out. Morrie worried about her, because he felt laughter is good medicine and a cartoonist has to be relaxed instead of being "uptight" when working.

Sometimes Letha worried a little about Morrie. "He's an eternal ham," she told her mother. "He not only teaches, he dramatizes everything."

School officials and people from many different places heard about Morrie and asked him to teach or lecture. At San Mateo (California) Junior College he became a team teacher with Jim Brown, cartoonist from San Francisco, and Ed Mitchell, a gag writer from San Carlos.

Morrie's mother was pleased when he was asked to be a guest speaker in the pulpit at Park Chapel Methodist Church. "I knew Morrie could do it," she beamed.

Morrie himself admitted he enjoyed being asked to give courses at colleges and universities. "And me, only a high school graduate with a few college credits."

Portland University asked him to be "artist in residence" during Black History Week in 1974 and Ohio State University invited him to be a lecturer at its summer journalism seminar the same year. Sometimes Morrie felt like a Ping-Pong ball, bouncing from one place to another.

But he always went back to his drawing board in Berkeley, to keep a steady supply of new "Wee Pals" strips ready.

When Morrie served on the White House Conference on Children as cochairman of the Child Development and Mass Media Section, he never dreamed that his "Wee Pals" would one day be TV characters. But as the popularity of his kids grew, TV producers saw them as program material.

Morrie was invited to do a special on the unity of the races, which he called "Kid Power," with "Wee Pals" as actors.

Oliver, Randy, Rocky, George, Jerry, Nipper, Connie, Wellington, Ralph, and even the dog, General Lee, appeared. Discrimination is what we don't need, the kids reminded viewers. Two records made especially for the show provided musical background with kids' voices singing, "Do You Know What It Means?" and "Pollution of the Mind."

Fan mail poured into the station and reviewers praised the show. As a result, Morrie was asked to do thirteen regular weekly shows.

"Kid Power," with animated "Wee Pals," became a nationally televised Saturday morning show. Morrie released the rights for the use of his kid characters.

KGO-TV, a San Francisco Bay area station, asked Morrie to do a series about "Wee Pals on the Go," and wanted him to be the commentator for the show. "We want kids, real live ones, doing interesting things that kids at home can watch on their TV screens."

Seventy-six children from a San Francisco theatrical agency were interviewed before six were found who matched the "Wee Pals" in appearance and racial background.

Kids and their parents enjoyed the show and "Wee Pals on the Go" ran for two seasons, totaling a year on television.

Now, even kids who couldn't read could see and hear "Wee Pals" right in their homes, and buy records of their songs to play and learn.

It was a long detour from his drawing board, Morrie felt. But just as his "Wee Pals" told about getting along and being friends with all races and doing fun things, he was happy.

The Oakland Symphony became popular *and* understandable when Morrie introduced the orchestra through "Wee Pals."

Chapter 9

NEW DECADES

Looking back at the years since "Wee Pals" was born, Morrie has to admit that they got around beyond his fondest dreams. They are in more than a dozen books. They boost the United States Department of Agriculture school lunch program on posters and television. They stressed children's safety in an Atlanta, Georgia, TV series, "Morrie's Minutes."

Working with the late Calvin Simmons, a young black music director and conductor of the Oakland (California) symphony, Morrie featured his "Wee Pals" in a booklet called "Make Friends With Music." Given to young concert audiences, the booklet introduces musical instruments in simple language and with imagery children understand. For three years, Morrie Concerts—during which his booklet was projected on a large screen behind the orchestra—were given so that youngsters could better see and understand, as well as hear, the programs. Later, these concerts were repeated with the San Mateo (California) Symphony.

Among Morrie's latest achievements is the illustration of a paperback book, *Oakland the Accessible City*, published by the Mayor's Commission on Disabled Persons. Using Charlotte, his "Wee Pals" wheelchair-occupant character, and adult figures representing the hearing impaired, the visually disabled, and the small in stature, Morrie illustrates how municipalities can include facilities in public buildings that, with other aids, will enable those with physical disabilities to participate in all aspects of civic affairs. The book has been widely circulated throughout the United States as an example of how other areas can become accessible cities for physically impaired residents and visitors.

Morrie's "Wee Pals" kids have also appeared in videotapes, on calendars and posters, in television spots, and in other books treating such subjects as prevention of child molestation and kidnapping, occupations and job qualifications, crime prevention, good nutrition, early childhood education, and sickle cell anemia.

Morrie now is a grandfather, and his four grandchildren provide added inspiration for his integrated strip and for his community activities on behalf of children. Granddaughter Michele has been added to the "Wee Pals" strip under the name of Mikki. Although his other grandchildren—Nicole, Morrie III, and Nathan—are not identified by name in the strip, their antics add spice to the daily goings-on.

Also added to the "Wee Pals" family over the years have been Pablo, a Latino; wheelchair-bound Charlotte and her pet parrot; and Thrin, a Vietnamese kid.

Morrie's family is proud of his lifelong accomplishments. Latest among them is inclusion of "Wee Pals" in the European edition of *Stars and Stripes*. This particularly warms Morrie's heart, feeling his "Wee Pals" are a link from home to servicemen overseas.

Always excited about tomorrow, Morrie admits he's still trying for "at least three new ideas a day." Pointing to his thick hair, Morrie says, "A guy can get gray here, but he can't rust inside the skull."

To all kids, Morrie says, "A person has to keep following his dreams as long as he lives."

He's humbly grateful that his father's hope of "a name of your own" for his sons has come true for him.

Letha accompanies Morrie as he receives another award—this time from the Boys Clubs of Oakland.

SOME MINIBIOGRAPHIES

Ira Aldridge (1805?-1867), actor; successful in England and Germany in Shakespearean roles such as *Othello*, *King Lear*, and *Macbeth*

Crispus Attucks (1723?-1770), leader of mob in Boston Massacre, March 5, 1770; one of three men killed by British troops

Max Baer (1909-1959), heavyweight boxing champion; knocked out Primo Carnera in 1934

Benjamin Banneker (1731-1806), inventor, mathematician, and astronomer; helped survey site of District of Columbia; defended intellectual equality of blacks in correspondence with Thomas Jefferson

Mary Bethune (1875-1955), educator; opened small school in Daytona Beach, Florida, in 1904, which merged with Cookman College in 1923 to become Bethune-Cookman College; adviser to Presidents Franklin D. Roosevelt and Harry S. Truman

James Cagney (1904-   ), movie actor famous for brash, sadistic, tough roles

E. Sims Campbell (1906-1971), cartoonist famous for his creation of "Esky" in *Esquire* magazine; depicted the world of high society, wine, women, and song; illustrated many poems by Langston Hughes

George Washington Carver (1864-1943), botanist known especially for his research on the industrial uses of peanuts

Joan Ganz Cooney (1929-   ), founder of the Children's Television Workshop; developer of the prize-winning children's program, "Sesame Street"

Colonel Benjamin Davis (1877-1970), army officer; first black to graduate from West Point

Frederick Douglass (1817?-1895), lecturer, traveler, and writer; founded an abolitionist newspaper, the *North Star*; helped recruit black regiments in Civil War; U.S. minister to Haiti, 1889-1891

101

Dr. Charles Drew (1904-1950), physician who developed efficient way to store plasma in blood banks

W.E.B. DuBois (1863-1963), educator, editor, and writer; professor of sociology, Atlanta University (from 1932); editor-in-chief of *Encyclopedia Africana*; editor of *Atlanta University Studies of the Negro Problem* (1897-1911), and *Crisis* (1910-1932)

Jean Baptiste Point du Sable (c.1750-1818), pioneer trader and first black settler in Chicago, 1779

Billy Eckstine (1914-   ), pop singer

John Fischetti (1916-1980), Pulitzer Prize-winning cartoonist for the *Chicago Daily News*

James Montgomery Flagg (1877-1960), painter, illustrator, and author; contributed to *St. Nicholas, Judge,* and *Life*

Dick Gregory (1932-   ), entertainer and black activist

W.C. Handy (1873-1958), musician and composer; wrote "St. Louis Blues"; called "father of the blues"

Matthew Henson (1866-1955), member of Peary's 1908 expedition to the North Pole; placed U.S. flag at the pole

Bill Holman, cartoonist who contributed to *Colliers, Saturday Evening Post, Life,* and *Judge*; had a lifelong love for and interest in firemen; developed the character of "Smokey Stover"

Langston Hughes (1902-1967), poet and writer; many of his works have been set to music

Bil Keane (1922-   ), staff member of *Stars and Stripes*; creator of the panel series, "At Ease with the Japanese," as well as two other popular series: "The Family Circus" and "Channel Chuckles"

John Henry Lewis (1914-1974), light heavyweight boxing champion, 1935-1939

Bill Mauldin (1921-   ), depicted squalid life of the GI in World War II in Pulitzer-winning cartoons that appeared in *Stars and Stripes* and elsewhere

Willard Mullins (1902-1978), sports cartoonist who created the "Bums" as a trademark for the Brooklyn Dodgers and contributed to *Life, Look, Time, Newsweek,* and the *Saturday Evening Post*

Bill Pickett, a black cowboy with the Lewis and Clark expedition, 1804-1806; called the "Dusty Demon from Texas"

Ernie Pyle (1900-1945), journalist who depicted the lives and hopes of ordinary citizens; the most popular correspondent of World War II, who wrote of ordinary enlisted men rather than officers

Hiram R. Revels (1822-1901), first black senator elected in Mississippi, served 1870-1871

Andy Rooney (1919-   ), writer and columnist; author of a history of *Stars and Stripes* and *Air Gunner;* contributor to the CBS-TV program, "60 Minutes"

Theodore Roosevelt (1858-1919), 26th president of the U.S., elected in 1912; winner of the Nobel Prize for Peace, 1906

Calvin Simmons, musician and conductor of the Oakland Symphony

Jack Tippitt (1923-   ), developer of the popular daily gag feature, "Amy"; contributor to *Look, Saturday Evening Post,* and *New Yorker;* past president of the National Cartoonists Society

Sojourner Truth (1797-1883), born Isabella Baumfree; preacher, abolitionist; raised funds for the Union in the Civil War; fought for black educational opportunities

Booker T. Washington (1856-1915), educator; born a slave; established Tuskegee Institute; gained national recognition as educational leader of black people in the U.S.

Alexander Wolcott (1887-1943), author and critic; drama critic for *New York World* (1925-1928) and *New York Times* (1914-1922)

Morrie Turner 1923-

1923 Morrie Turner is born in Oakland, California. The first sound-on-film motion picture, *Phonofilm*, is shown by Lee de Forest at a New York City theater.

1924 A law is approved by Congress making all American Indians citizens. George Gershwin writes *Rhapsody in Blue*.

1925 John T. Scopes is found guilty of teaching evolution in a Dayton, Tennessee, high school.

1926 Dr. Robert H. Goddard demonstrates the practicality of rockets. The Air Commerce Act is passed, providing federal aid for airlines and airports.

1927 Captain Charles A. Lindberg flies the *Spirit of St. Louis* on first nonstop New York-Paris flight. Al Jolson stars in *The Jazz Singer*, the first talking picture.

1928 Herbert Hoover is elected president.

1929 The stock market crash marks the end of postwar prosperity as stock prices plummet. Worldwide economic crisis follows.

1930 More than 1,300 U.S. banks close. Hitler's Nazi party gains a majority in German elections.

1931 The Empire State Building opens in New York City.

1932 Franklin D. Roosevelt wins a landslide victory in presidential election. The number of unemployed in the U.S. reaches 12,000,000.

1933 U.S. passes the Twenty-first Amendment, repealing Prohibition. In the "100 days" session of Congress, New Deal social and economic measures are passed.

1934 Max Baer wins the heavyweight boxing championship.

1935 John Henry Lewis wins the light heavyweight boxing championship. The Social Security Act is passed by Congress. Gershwin's *Porgy and Bess* opens.

1936 Boulder Dam is completed. Margaret Mitchell publishes *Gone with the Wind*. Roosevelt is reelected. Benjamin Oliver Davis, Jr., is first black to graduate from West Point.

1937 Amelia Earhart's plane is lost in the Pacific. Roosevelt asks for six additional Supreme Court justices, but the "packing plan" is defeated.

1938 National minimum wage is enacted. Orson Welles's radio program, *War of the Worlds*, causes mass hysteria.

1939 New York World's Fair opens. Albert Einstein alerts President Roosevelt to A-bomb opportunity. John Steinbeck publishes *Grapes of Wrath*. The Nazi-Soviet nonaggression pact frees Germany to attack Poland. Britain and France declare war on Germany. U.S. declares its neutrality.

1940 U.S. authorizes sale of surplus war material to Britain. First peacetime draft is approved. Richard Wright publishes *Native Son*.

1941 The Four Freedoms are termed essential by President Roosevelt in speech to Congress. The Lend-Lease Act is signed providing military credits to Britain and aid to the USSR. The Atlantic Charter is signed by Roosevelt and Winston Churchill. The Japanese attack Pearl Harbor. U.S. declares was on Germany and Japan.

1942 Japanese-Americans are moved to West Coast detention camps. Marines land at Guadalcanal. First nuclear chain reaction is produced at the University of Chicago. Japan suffers major defeat at Midway Island.

1943 All war contractors are barred from racial discrimination. Roosevelt signs the pay-as-you-go income tax bill. In Detroit 34 people are killed at race riot; six are killed at race riot in Harlem.

1944 Allied forces invade Europe at Normandy beachhead. G.I. Bill of Rights providing benefits for veterans is signed.

1945 Roosevelt, Churchill, and Joseph Stalin meet at Yalta. Marines land on Iwo Jima. Roosevelt dies of cerebral hemorrhage. Harry S. Truman becomes president. Germany surrenders. Atomic bomb is dropped on Hiroshima and Nagasaki in Japan. Japan surrenders.

1946 400,000 U.S. mine workers strike. Other industries follow. The Phillipines given independence by the U.S.

1947 Jackie Robinson becomes first black baseball player in the big leagues when he joins the Brooklyn Dodgers. Secretary of State George Marshall proposes the European Recovery Program (the "Marshall Plan"). Morrie Turner earns first freelance check for cartoon for Baker's Helper magazine.

1948 Organization of American States is founded. Harry S. Truman is elected president.

1949 North Atlantic Treaty Organization (NATO) is founded. Eleven Communists in the U.S. are convicted of conspiracy to overthrow the government.

1950 Senator Joseph McCarthy charges that Communists have infiltrated the U.S. government. Truman authorizes production of the H-bomb. Korean War begins. U.S. sends military advisers to South Vietnam.

1951 Color television is introduced into the U.S. Congress passes Twenty-second Amendment limiting presidency to two terms. Korean cease-fire talks begin. Japanese Peace Treaty signed in San Francisco.

1952 Immigration and Naturalization Act is passed eliminating the last racial and ethnic barriers to immigration. Dwight D. Eisenhower is elected president. Korean armistice ends the war.

1953 Joseph Stalin dies. Nikita Khrushchev becomes head of the Central Committee of the Soviet Communist party.

1954 First atomic-powered submarine—the Nautilus—is launched. Racial segregation in the schools is ruled unconstitutional by the Supreme Court as a violation of the Fourteenth Amendment. Senator McCarthy leads televised hearings into alleged Communist influence in the army.

1955 Supreme Court orders that there be "all deliberate speed" in integrating public schools. Rosa Parks refuses to give her seat on the bus to a white man. Bus segregation is declared unconstitutional by a federal court. U.S. agrees to help train South Vietnamese army.

1956 Massive resistance to Supreme Court desegregation rulings is called for by 101 southern congressmen. Soviet troops invade Hungary.

1957 Congress approves first civil rights bill for blacks since the Reconstruction to protect voting rights. National guard called out by Arkansas Governor Orval Faubus to bar nine black students from entering all-white high school in Little Rock. Eisenhower sends federal troops to enforce court order. Soviets launch first man-made satellites.

1958 First domestic jet airline service is opened between New York and Miami. First U.S. earth satellite goes into orbit. Five thousand U.S. marines sent to Lebanon to protect elected government from overthrow.

1959 Hawaii and Alaska become states. Fidel Castro overthrows Cuban dictator Fulgencio Batista and becomes president.

1960 Morrie Turner becomes delegate to White House Conference on Children. A wave of sit-ins begins when four black college students in Greensboro, North Carolina, refuse to move from a Woolworth lunch counter when they are denied service. Congress approves a strong voting rights act. John F. Kennedy defeats Nixon for the presidency.

1961 U.S. severs diplomatic relations with Cuba. Invasion of Cuba's Bay of Pigs is repulsed. Commander Alan Shepard is rocketed above the earth in the first manned suborbital flight.

1962 Lieutenant Colonel John H. Glenn, Jr., becomes first astronaut to orbit the earth. James Meredith becomes first black student at University of Mississippi. U.S. sends military advisers to South Vietnam.

1963 Morrie Turner becomes the first black member of the Northern California Cartoonists and Gag Writers and attends the conference in San Francisco. Two hundred thousand people demonstrate in Washington in support of black demands for equal rights. Martin Luther King, Jr., gives his "I Have a Dream" speech. President John F. Kennedy is assassinated. Lyndon B. Johnson becomes president.

1964 Morrie Turner's cartoon, "Wee Pals," is syndicated. Omnibus civil rights bill is passed banning discrimination in voting, jobs, public accommodations, etc. Three civil rights workers reported missing in Mississippi and are found buried in August; twenty-one white men are arrested. U.S. Congress passes Tonkin Resolution authorizing presidential action in Vietnam.

1965 New Voting Rights Act signed. Riots in Watts, the black section of Los Angeles, result in thirty-five deaths and $200 million property damage. The U.S. forces in Vietnam number over 180,000. Antiwar demonstrations sweep the U.S.

1966 Edward Brooke, the first black senator in eighty-five years, is elected in Massachusetts. The Medicare program, health care for Americans over sixty-five, is inaugurated.

1967 Morrie Turner goes to entertain the troops in Vietnam. Thurgood Marshall is sworn in as first black Supreme Court Justice. Carl D. Stokes (Democrat, Cleveland) and Richard G. Hatcher (Democrat, Gary, Indiana) are elected first black mayors of major American cities. Black riots in Newark, New Jersey, and Detroit, Michigan, leave many dead, injured, and homeless. U.S. bombs Hanoi, North Vietnam. Fifty thousand demonstrate against the Vietnam War at the Lincoln Memorial in Washington, D.C.

1968 Morrie Turner receives the Brotherhood Award of the National Conference of Christians and Jews. Martin Luther King, Jr., is assassinated. Robert Kennedy is assassinated. President Johnson curbs the bombing of North Vietnam. Richard M. Nixon is elected president.

1969 Morrie Turner receives the B'nai B'rith Anti-Defamation League Humanitarian Award and the Northern California Award of Merit. Turner publishes *The Black and White Coloring Book*. Neil Armstrong is the first man to walk on the moon. Anti-Vietnam War demonstrations reach their peak as 250,000 march on Washington.

1970 Morrie Turner publishes *Nipper's Secret Power*. Four students at Kent State University are shot by National Guard during antiwar demonstrations. Two women generals, the first in U.S. history, are named by President Nixon.

1971 People's Republic of China is admitted to the United Nations. The Twenty-sixth Amendment lowering the voting age to eighteen is passed. U.S. forces in Vietnam are reduced to 140,000.

1972 Morrie Turner publishes *God Is Groovy*. Nixon is reelected president; he reinstates diplomatic relations with China, and is the first president to visit China and Moscow. Burglers break into the Democratic headquarters at the Watergate Hotel in Washington, D.C.

1973 Nixon aides H.R. Haldeman, John D. Erlichman, John Dean, and Richard Kleindienst resign amid charges of White House efforts to obstruct justice in the Watergate case. Vietnam peace pacts signed in Paris. House Judiciary Committee begins impeachment hearings. Vice-president Spiro Agnew resigns in income tax scandal; Gerald Ford becomes vice-president. Middle East unrest causes oil prices to rise and signals an energy crisis.

1974 Nixon resigns presidency. Gerald Ford becomes president and pardons Nixon. Arabs lift oil embargo.

1975 South Vietnam surrenders to North Vietnam. The war ends.

1976 The U.S. celebrates its bicentennial. Jimmy Carter is elected president. U.S. and U.S.S.R. sign a nuclear arms limitation treaty.

1977 President Carter pardons about ten thousand Vietnam draft evaders.

1978 Morrie Turner publishes *Kid Power* and *Welcome to the Club*.

1979 Some ninety people, including sixty-three Americans, are taken hostage at the U.S. embassy in Teheran, Iran, by followers of the Ayatollah Khomeini who demanded the return of the Shah, who is undergoing medical treatment in New York. Sandra Day O'Conner becomes the first woman justice of the Supreme Court.

1980 Ronald Reagan is elected president of the United States. Morrie Turner publishes *All God's Chillun Got Soul*.

1981 Minutes after the inauguration of Ronald Reagan, the hostages are freed in Iran. The first reusable spacecraft, the space shuttle *Columbia*, is sent into space and completes its mission successfully.

1982 The shuttle *Columbia* completes its first operational flight. The Senate votes 57-37 in favor of a bill that virtually eliminates busing for the purposes of racial integration. A retired dentist, Dr. Barney B. Clark, becomes the first recipient of an artificial heart.

1983 Sally Ride becomes the first woman to travel in space. The Supreme Court holds that the Internal Revenue Service can deny tax exemption to schools that practice racial discrimination. The third Monday in January is declared a national holiday honoring Martin Luther King, Jr.

INDEX- *Page numbers in boldface type indicate illustrations.*

110

ABOUT THE AUTHOR

Mary Kentra Ericsson has spent most of her life with her fingers on a typewriter. She is the author of three other books: *Ragusan Bride: Dubrovnik to San Francisco*, *Flying Feathers*, and *Glasses for Gladys*. She also has written the television narration of Pittsburg's Living History, numerous magazine articles and stories, and The Glory Years, a newspaper column on aging.

Ericsson was a newspaper reporter for twenty years, was employed in school and hospital public relations, and recently retired after sixteen years of teaching a creative writing course for Pittsburg Adult School. A native of San Francisco, and a resident of Pittsburg, California, she is a member of California Writers Club and is on the board of directors of its Berkeley branch. She has three sons, three grandsons, and a great grandson.